BEWARE! KILLER PLANTS

CARNIVOROUS PLANTS

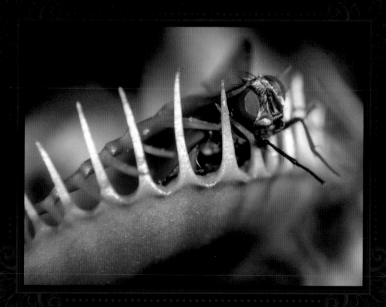

by Joyce Markovics

CHERRY LAKE PRESS

Ann Arbor, Michigan

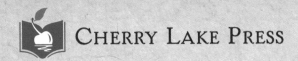

CHERRY LAKE PRESS

Published in the United States of America by Cherry Lake Publishing Group
Ann Arbor, Michigan
www.cherrylakepublishing.com

Reading Adviser: Beth Walker Gambro, MS Ed., Reading Consultant, Yorkville, IL
Content Adviser: Angie Andrade, Senior Horticulturist, Denver Botanic Gardens
Book Designer: Ed Morgan

Photo Credits: © Patila/Shutterstock, cover and title page; Wikimedia Commons, 4; © Ernie Cooper/Shutterstock, 5 top; © Lost_in_the_Midwest/Shutterstock, 5 bottom; © Ernie Cooper/Shutterstock, 6 top; © Papik/Shutterstock, 6 bottom; © Kuttelvaserova Stuchelova/Shutterstock, 7; © nico99/Shutterstock, 8; © Alexandra Kovaleva/Shutterstock, 8–9; © Anna Sereno Garrison/Shutterstock, 10; © Photogrape/Shutterstock, 11; © freepik.com, 12 left; © Kelly Marken/Shutterstock, 12 right; © Jeff Holcombe/Shutterstock, 13; © COULANGES/Shutterstock, 14; © goran_safarek/Shutterstock, 15 top; Michal Rubes, Wikimedia Commons, 15 bottom; © D. Kucharski K. Kucharska/Shutterstock, 16; © goran_safarek/Shutterstock, 17 top; © freepik.com, 17 bottom; © Luka Hercigonja/Shutterstock, 18; © JIANG TIANMU/Shutterstock, 19 top; © Serge Goujon/Shutterstock, 19 bottom; Michal Rubes, Wikimedia Commons, 20; © BMJ/Shutterstock, 21; © MerlinTuttle.org, 22.

Cherry Lake Press is an imprint of Cherry Lake Publishing Group.

Library of Congress Cataloging-in-Publication Data

Names: Markovics, Joyce L., author.
Title: Carnivorous plants / by Joyce Markovics.
Description: Ann Arbor, Michigan : Cherry Lake Publishing, [2021] | Series: Beware! killer plants | Includes bibliographical references and index. | Audience: Grades 4–6
Identifiers: LCCN 2021001368 (print) | LCCN 2021001369 (ebook) | ISBN 9781534187665 (hardcover) | ISBN 9781534189065 (paperback) | ISBN 9781534190467 (pdf) | ISBN 9781534191860 (ebook)
Subjects: LCSH: Carnivorous plants—Juvenile literature.
Classification: LCC QK917 M35 2021 (print) | LCC QK917 (ebook) | DDC 583/.887—dc23
LC record available at https://lccn.loc.gov/2021001368
LC ebook record available at https://lccn.loc.gov/2021001369

Printed in the United States of America
Corporate Graphics

CONTENTS

A TRICKY TRAP

It's a sunny day in a North Carolina bog. A grasshopper hops toward a Venus flytrap. The plant has leaves that are hinged in the middle like jaws. The insect can't resist the sweet nectar on the leaves. Little does it know that it's about to enter a trap.

A Venus flytrap

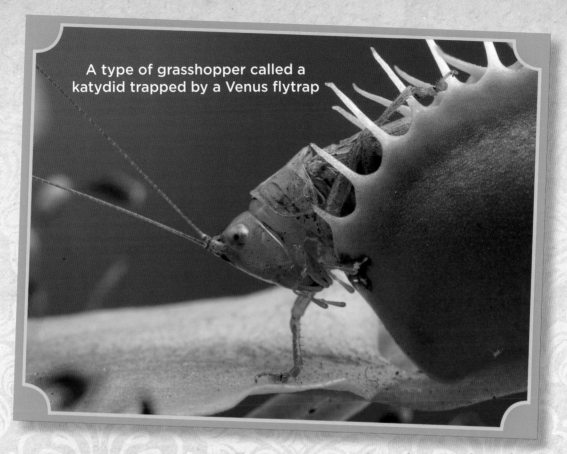

A type of grasshopper called a katydid trapped by a Venus flytrap

The grasshopper inches closer to the plant. It brushes against tiny trigger hairs on the surface of a hinged leaf. Suddenly, the leaf springs shut!

A bog is a wet, marshy area of land. Venus flytraps only grow in bogs in North Carolina and South Carolina.

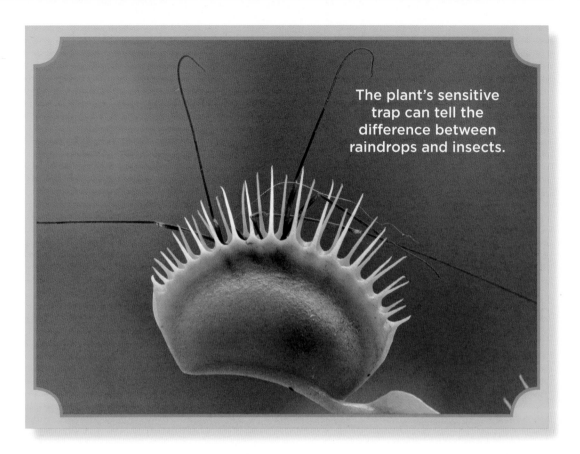

The plant's sensitive trap can tell the difference between raindrops and insects.

The grasshopper struggles to move. But it's trapped. As many as 20 cilia extend from the leaf's edges. These long spines stop the grasshopper from escaping. The trap closes tighter. Next, glands on the inside of the leaf begin to ooze digestive juices.

The juices drown the unlucky bug. Then they begin to dissolve its body! This process takes 5 to 12 days. The Venus flytrap then absorbs the nutrients from the insect's dead body.

This fly tries to wiggle out of the plant's trap. But the cilia lock together, trapping the bug.

Most plants get all the nutrients they need from the soil and the sun. Venus flytraps and other **carnivorous** plants are different. Why? These meat-eating plants often grow in wet **habitats** where the soil is poor.

A Venus flytrap may only eat a few bugs in its entire life.

Poor soil has few nutrients, such as nitrogen. Plants need nitrogen to thrive. Carnivorous plants get a boost of nitrogen and other nutrients by eating animals. Over time, these killer plants have developed clever ways to trap their prey.

Carnivorous plants don't get all of their nutrients from bugs. Like other plants, carnivorous plants perform photosynthesis. They use energy from the sun to make their own food.

PITCHER PLANTS

Venus flytraps are just one of 15 major groups of carnivorous plants. The plants come in an amazing variety of shapes and sizes. Pitcher plants make up one of the biggest and most striking groups. Some pitcher plants look like hanging cups. Others are like tall, slim vases.

This type of pitcher plant is called a cobra lily because it resembles a snake with a forked tongue.

All pitcher plants catch prey in a similar way—the pitfall trap. The leaves of a pitcher plant form a tube, or pitcher. It's open at the top and closed at the bottom. At the bottom is a pool of powerful digestive juices.

The digestive juices of a pitcher plant

At the top of the pitcher is part of a leaf that's shaped like a hood. The hood glistens with sugary nectar. Insects can't resist this sweet liquid. As they drink it, the bugs often lose their grip on the plant. *Splash!* Down they slide through the tube into the deadly pool.

A fly is attracted to a sweet-smelling pitcher plant.

The waxy walls of the pitcher are too slippery to climb. With nowhere to escape, the insects soon drown. Slowly, the bugs' bodies turn into a nitrogen-rich liquid. Through its leaves, the plant absorbs the insect soup.

A drowned fly inside a pitcher plant

Some pitcher plants are large enough to trap lizards and mice!

SUNDEWS AND BUTTERWORTS

The sundew plant has a sneaky method to catch prey. Insects that fly near it are drawn to the shiny drops on its pointy leaves. The drops look like sweet globs of nectar or dew. In fact, they're as sticky as superglue.

Spoon-leaved sundew plants are found mostly in Asia. But sundews grow in many places worldwide.

An up-close view of a sundew's sticky goo

Once a fly or other bug lands on the leaf, it gets stuck in the goo. The leaves then curl tightly around the bug, pushing it toward the plant's center. There, the sundew coats the bug in body-dissolving juices.

Sundews are among the smallest carnivorous plants. An entire pygmy sundew plant is about the size of a penny!

Like sundews, butterworts are sticky. But they move much more slowly. These plants look like the perfect landing pad for tiny insects. But when an insect touches down on a slippery, sticky leaf, the landing pad becomes a trap.

Butterwort plants make one of the strongest "glues" found in nature.

As the bug fights to free itself, thousands of glands in the butterwort's leaves release digestive juices. The leaves slowly form a hollow under the bug. The juices pool around the insect. They can start breaking down the insect's body while it's still alive!

An ant trapped by a butterwort

A butterwort's leaves feel greasy, as if they're coated in butter.

BLADDERWORTS

Bladderworts, another kind of carnivorous plant, trap prey in an entirely different way. These plants live in wet soil or water. They have underwater stems covered with bubblelike traps, or bladders. The bladders are only about the size of the head of a pin.

Bladderwort plants grow in Africa, Asia, Australia, and other parts of the world.

Each bladder has a kind of trapdoor that swings inward. Surrounding the trapdoor are tiny trigger hairs.

The bladderwort's branches and bubblelike bladders

Almost all carnivorous plants produce flowers. The flowers often grow on stalks far above the plants' deadly traps.

If a water flea or other tiny aquatic animal swims near the bladderwort, it can trigger the hairs. In just 15 milliseconds, the trapdoor swings inward. Water gushes into the bladder trap, sucking the insect inside. The trapped bug is now doomed to become dinner.

A bladderwort with its prey

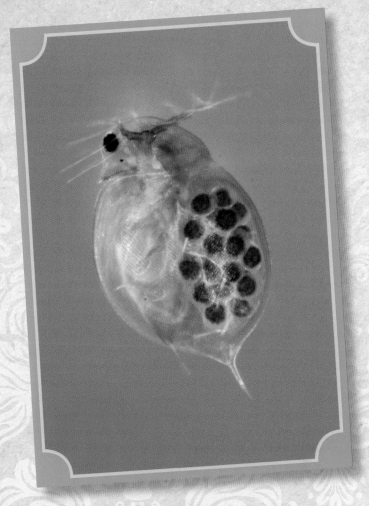

A water flea is about the same size as the period at the end of this sentence.

It isn't just small animals that are at risk. Some bladderworts are large enough to eat small fish. Bladderworts can reset their traps in about 30 minutes. This ability makes them the hungriest of all carnivorous plants. Beware—they're almost always ready to attack!

PLANT PARTNERS

Plants and animals sometimes help one another.
This type of relationship is called mutualism.

On the Asian island of Borneo, a Nepenthes pitcher plant has a bat partner. The Hardwicke's woolly bat hangs upside down inside the pitcher. This tight space is a shelter for the tiny bat to sleep and escape heavy rains. The bat roosts—and poops—inside the pitcher.

Nepenthes Pitcher Plant

The pitcher plant provides a safe, dry place for the bat to rest.

Hardwicke's Woolly Bat

The bat poops inside the pitcher plant. The poop provides more than one-third of the nitrogen the plant needs.

GLOSSARY

aquatic (uh-KWOT-ik) relating to water

carnivorous (kar-NIV-ur-uhss) meat-eating; carnivorous plants catch insects and other small animals to get nutrients

dew (DOO) small drops of water that collect overnight on cool surfaces

digestive juices (dye-JESS-tiv JOO-siz) liquids that help break down food so that a plant or animal can use it for energy

dissolve (di-ZOLV) to break down something into a liquid

glands (GLANDZ) plant or animal parts that produce chemicals

glistens (GLISS-uhns) reflects a sparkling light

habitats (HAB-uh-tats) places in the wild where plants and animals normally live

insect (IN-sekt) a small animal that has six legs, three main body parts, two antennas, and a hard covering called an exoskeleton

nectar (NEK-tur) a sweet liquid produced by plants

nutrients (NOO-tree-uhnts) substances needed by plants to grow and stay healthy; most plants take in nutrients from the soil; carnivorous plants get them by eating animals

prey (PRAY) an animal that is hunted by a plant or animal for food

trigger (TRIG-ur) something that brings about an action or process

Johnson, Rebecca L. *Carnivorous Plants*. Minneapolis: Lerner Publications, 2007.

Lawler, Janet. *Scary Plants*. New York: Penguin Young Readers, 2017.

Thorogood, Chris. *Perfectly Peculiar Plants*. Lake Forest, CA: Words & Pictures, 2018.

Websites

Atlanta Botanical Garden
   https://atlantabg.org/plan-your-visit/outdoor-collections/carnivorous-plants/

Kidspace Children's Museum: Carnivorous Plants
   https://kidspacemuseum.org/uncategorized/ask-kidspace-carnivorous-plants/

San Diego Zoo: Gotcha! Carnivorous Plants
   https://kids.sandiegozoo.org/stories/gotcha-carnivorous-plants

Index

About The Author

Joyce Markovics enjoys writing about and collecting unusual plants. One of her favorites is a 72-year-old miniature lemon tree that her grandfather planted from seed. Despite its small size, the tree produces monster lemons.

24